The Pit Pony's Tale

Written & Illustrated
By Tomos

'Welsh' - The last of the South Wales pit ponies pictured at Blaenserchan Colliery c.1985

© Tomos

First published in August 2012

All rights reserved

The right of Tomos
to be identified as author of this work has been asserted by him
in accordance with the Copyright Designs and Patents Act 1993.

ISBN 978-1-905967-39-1

Published in the U.K. by
Old Bakehouse Publications
Church Street, Abertillery, Gwent NP13 1EA
Telephone: 01495 212600 Fax: 01495 216222
Email: theoldbakeprint@btconnect.com
www: oldbakehouseprint.co.uk

Made and printed in the UK
by J.R. Davies (Printers) Ltd.

All rights reserved.
No part of this publication may be reproduced, stored in a retrieval system, or transmitted in any form
or by any means, electronic, mechanical, photocopying, recording or otherwise, without
the prior permission of the author and/or publishers.
For the avoidance of doubt, this includes reproduction of any image in this book on an internet site.

British Library Cataloguing in Publication Data: a catalogue
record for this book is available from the British Library.

Grateful thanks are extended to Six Bells Regeneration Ltd. for permission to use the image
of 'The Guardian of the Valleys' memorial.

10% of the profit of the sale of this edition of The Pit Pony's Tale
will be donated to 'The Mines Rescue Service'.

Mining

The poems and illustrations in this book have been inspired by coal mining during the Victorian era. During this time coal was the life-blood of a nation hungry for steam power. It brought people together, it brought wealth and it brought hard times.

Even in modern times miners face dangerous and hazardous conditions underground.

For
Frederick White
and all those who lost their lives in
the 1960 Explosion
at Six Bells Colliery,
South Wales.

The Door Boy

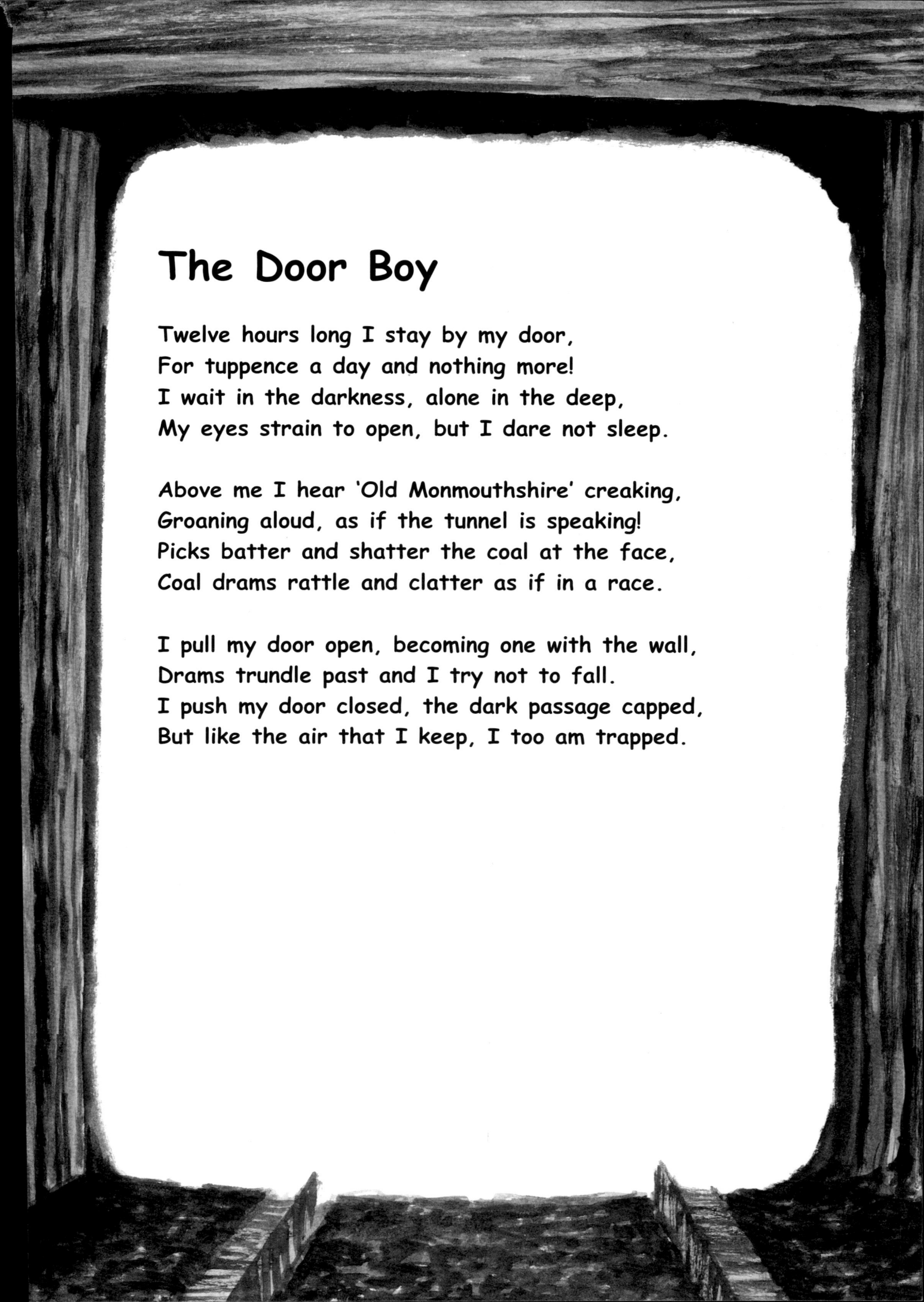

Twelve hours long I stay by my door,
For tuppence a day and nothing more!
I wait in the darkness, alone in the deep,
My eyes strain to open, but I dare not sleep.

Above me I hear 'Old Monmouthshire' creaking,
Groaning aloud, as if the tunnel is speaking!
Picks batter and shatter the coal at the face,
Coal drams rattle and clatter as if in a race.

I pull my door open, becoming one with the wall,
Drams trundle past and I try not to fall.
I push my door closed, the dark passage capped,
But like the air that I keep, I too am trapped.

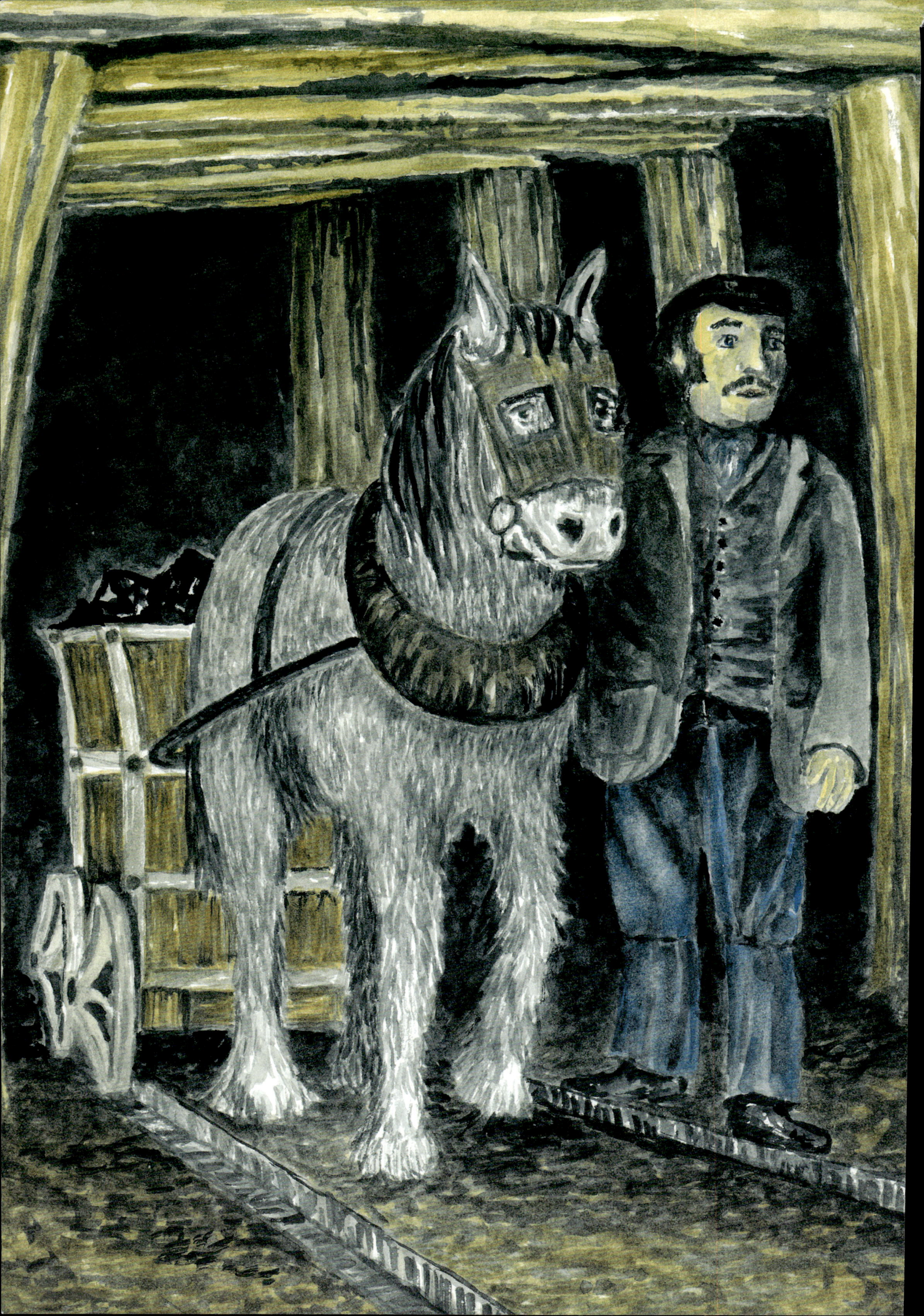

The Pit Pony's Tale

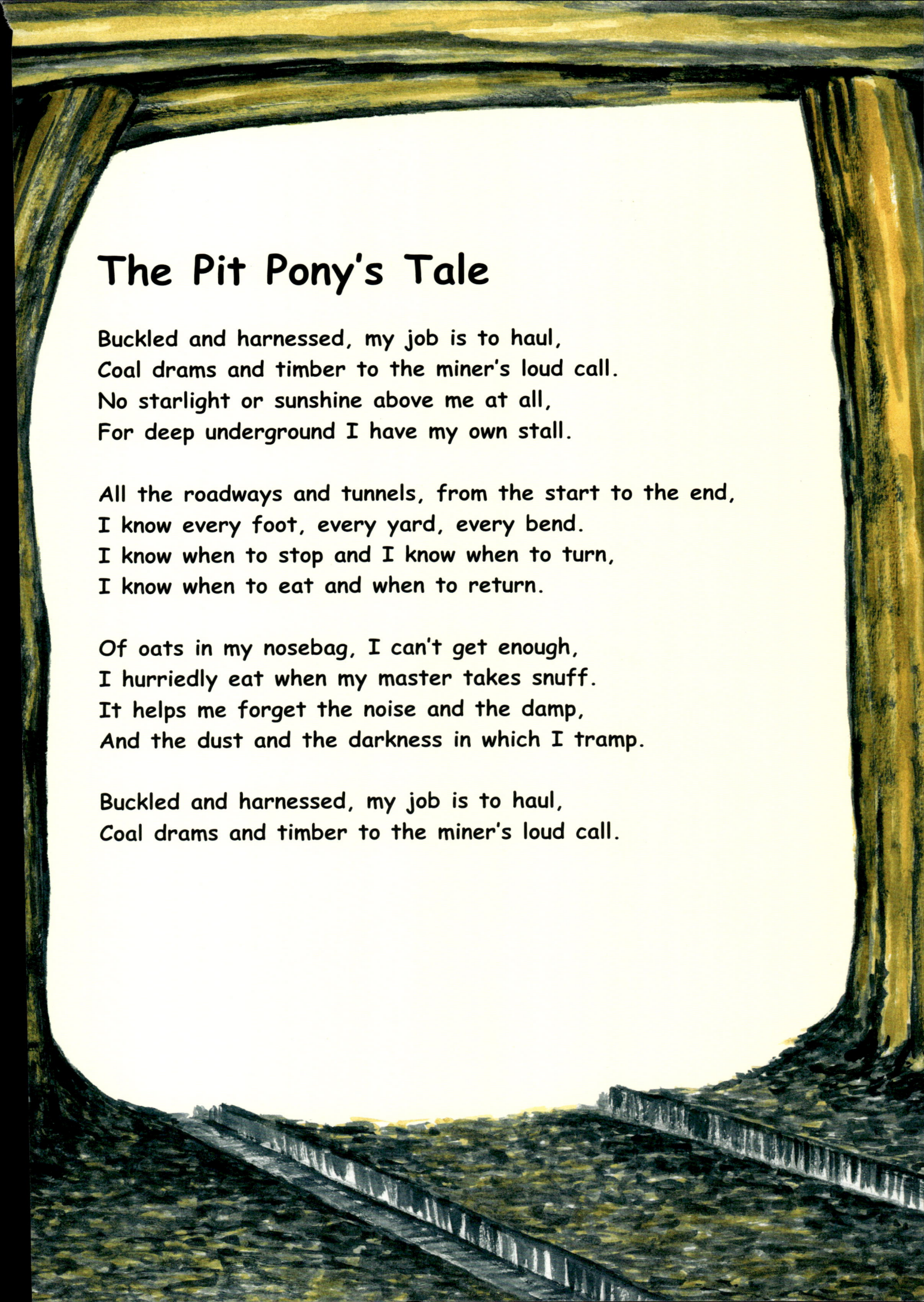

Buckled and harnessed, my job is to haul,
Coal drams and timber to the miner's loud call.
No starlight or sunshine above me at all,
For deep underground I have my own stall.

All the roadways and tunnels, from the start to the end,
I know every foot, every yard, every bend.
I know when to stop and I know when to turn,
I know when to eat and when to return.

Of oats in my nosebag, I can't get enough,
I hurriedly eat when my master takes snuff.
It helps me forget the noise and the damp,
And the dust and the darkness in which I tramp.

Buckled and harnessed, my job is to haul,
Coal drams and timber to the miner's loud call.

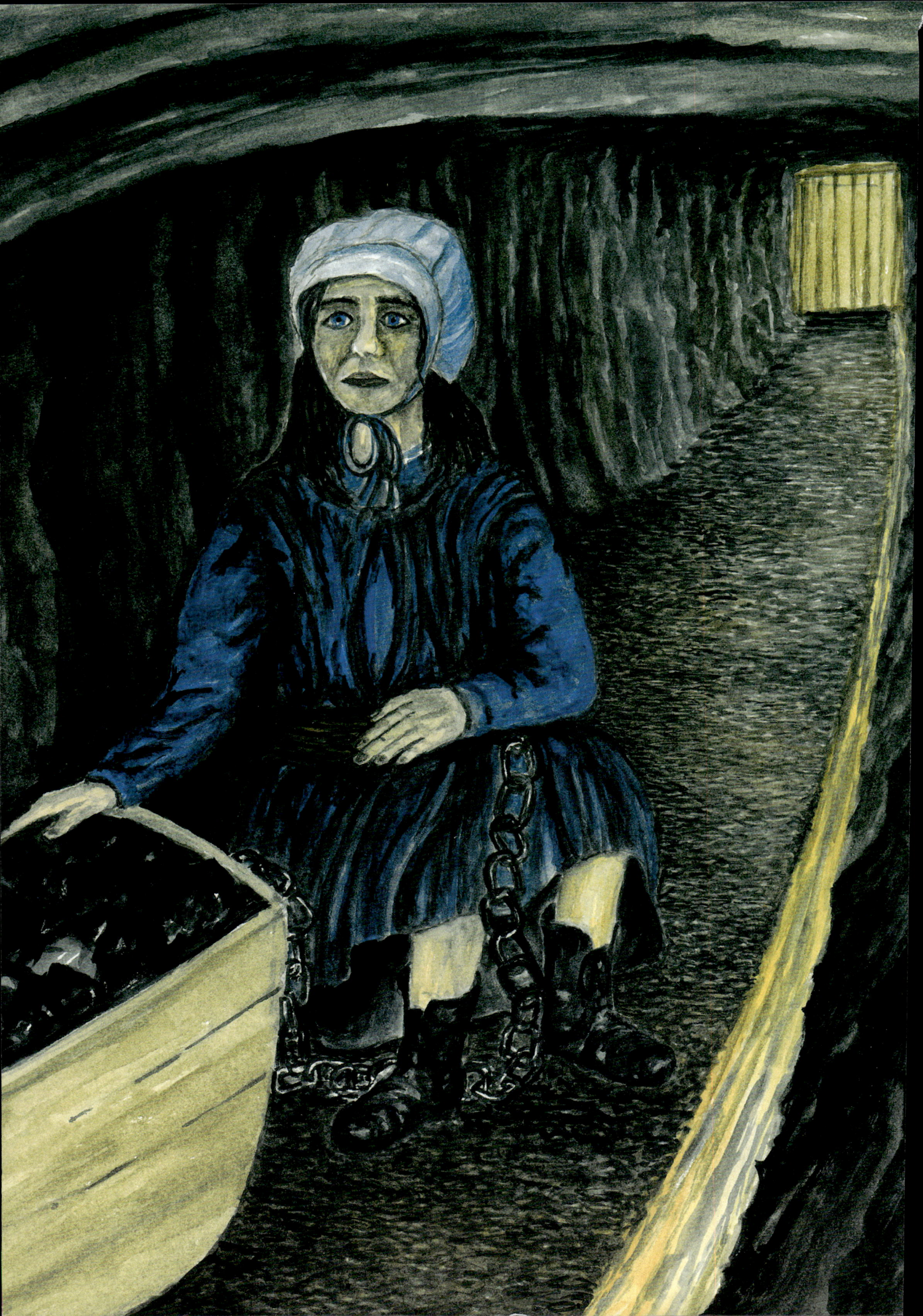

Tell Them Sir

Tell them Sir,
Tell them that it's not fair,
To make us go down pit without a care.

Tell them Sir
That the work is awful cruel,
That we'd be better off in school.

Tell them Sir,
That in the tunnel you can't stand at all,
That when we work, we have to crawl.

Tell them Sir,
Do tell them please,
Of the scars on our backs and the cuts on our knees.

Tell them Sir,
Tell them that it's not fair,
To make us go down pit without a care.

Inspiration - The Royal Commission Reports on Children in The Mines - 1842

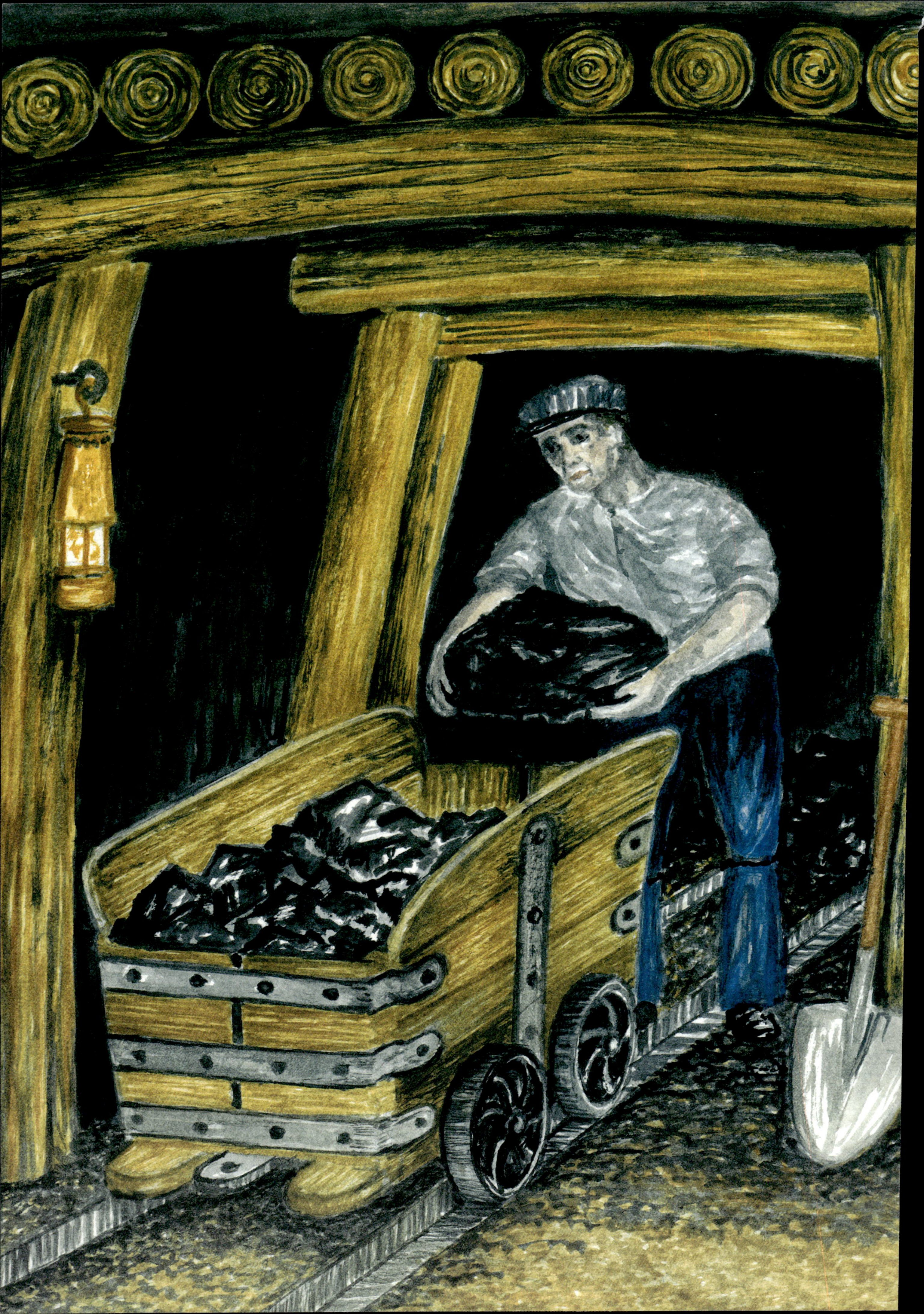

Loading For Me'Da

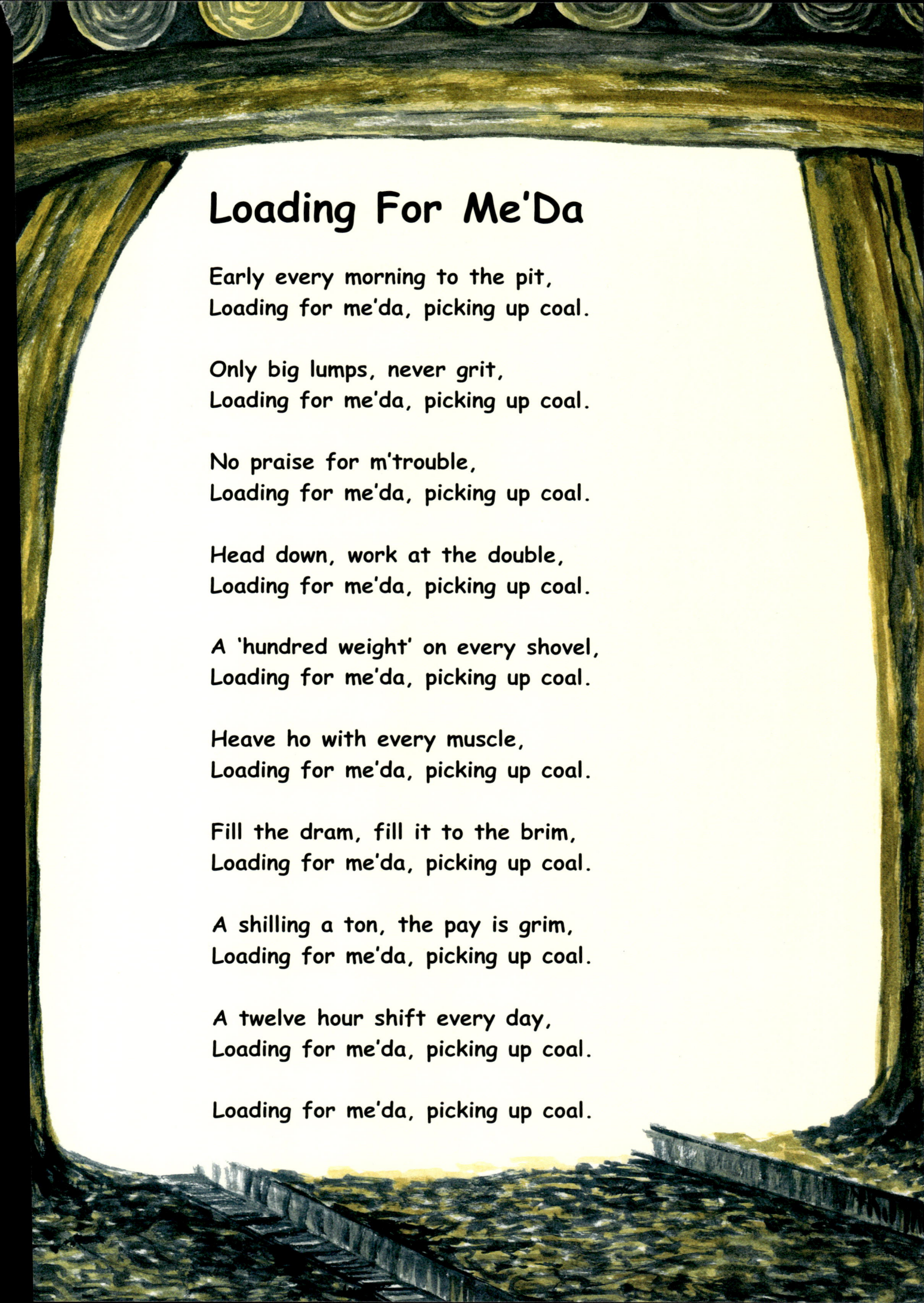

Early every morning to the pit,
Loading for me'da, picking up coal.

Only big lumps, never grit,
Loading for me'da, picking up coal.

No praise for m'trouble,
Loading for me'da, picking up coal.

Head down, work at the double,
Loading for me'da, picking up coal.

A 'hundred weight' on every shovel,
Loading for me'da, picking up coal.

Heave ho with every muscle,
Loading for me'da, picking up coal.

Fill the dram, fill it to the brim,
Loading for me'da, picking up coal.

A shilling a ton, the pay is grim,
Loading for me'da, picking up coal.

A twelve hour shift every day,
Loading for me'da, picking up coal.

Loading for me'da, picking up coal.

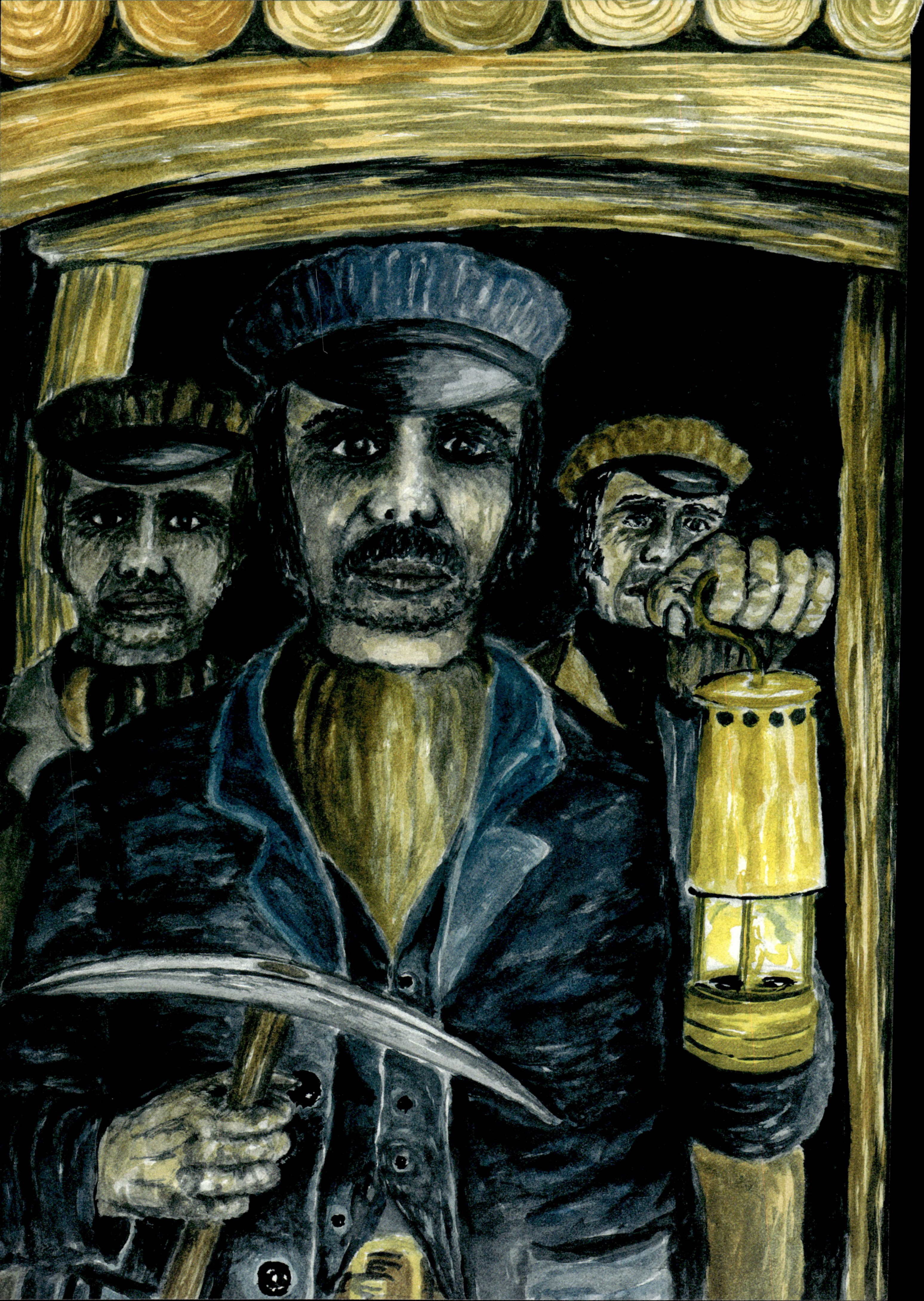

Davy Lamp

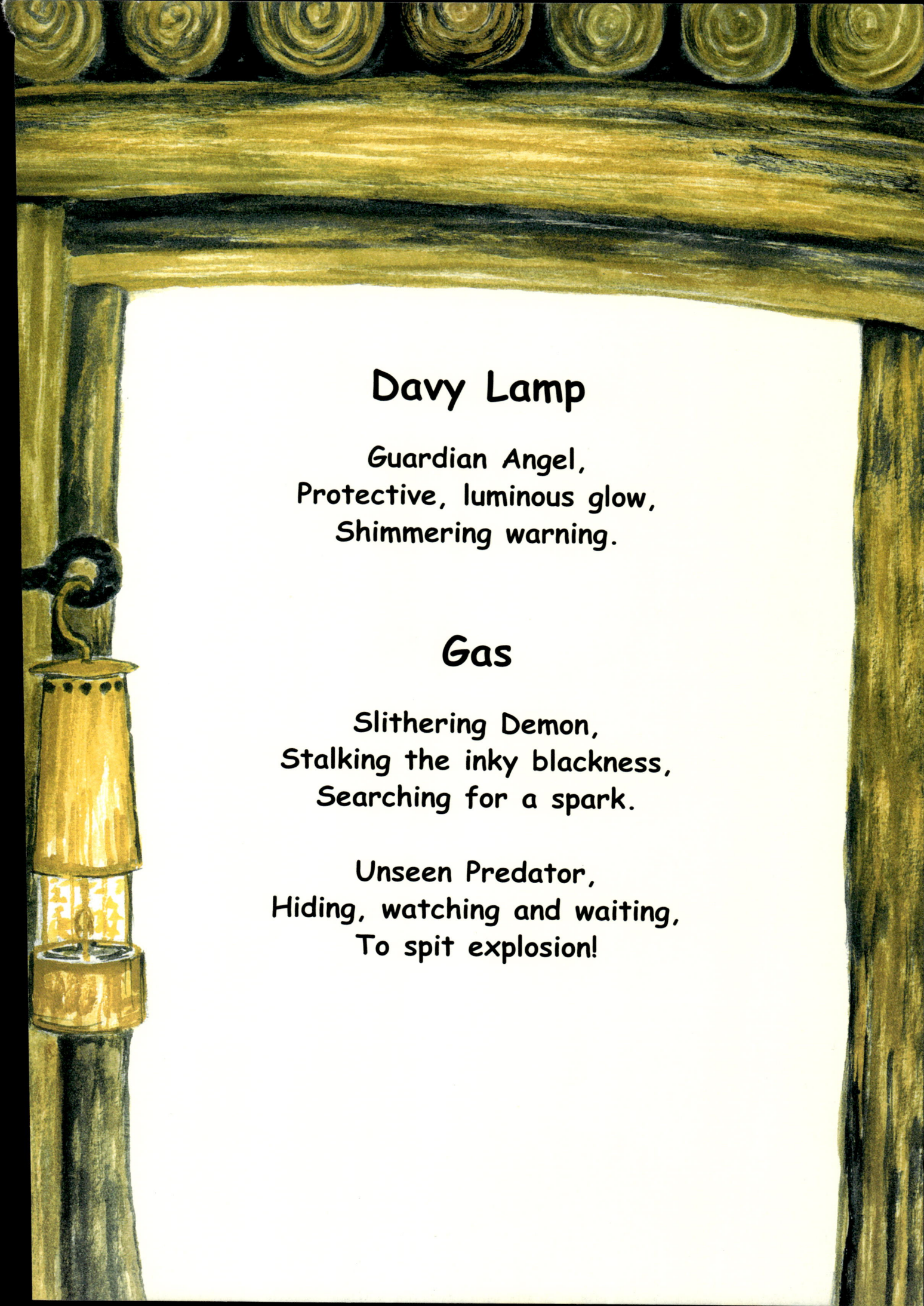

Guardian Angel,
Protective, luminous glow,
Shimmering warning.

Gas

Slithering Demon,
Stalking the inky blackness,
Searching for a spark.

Unseen Predator,
Hiding, watching and waiting,
To spit explosion!

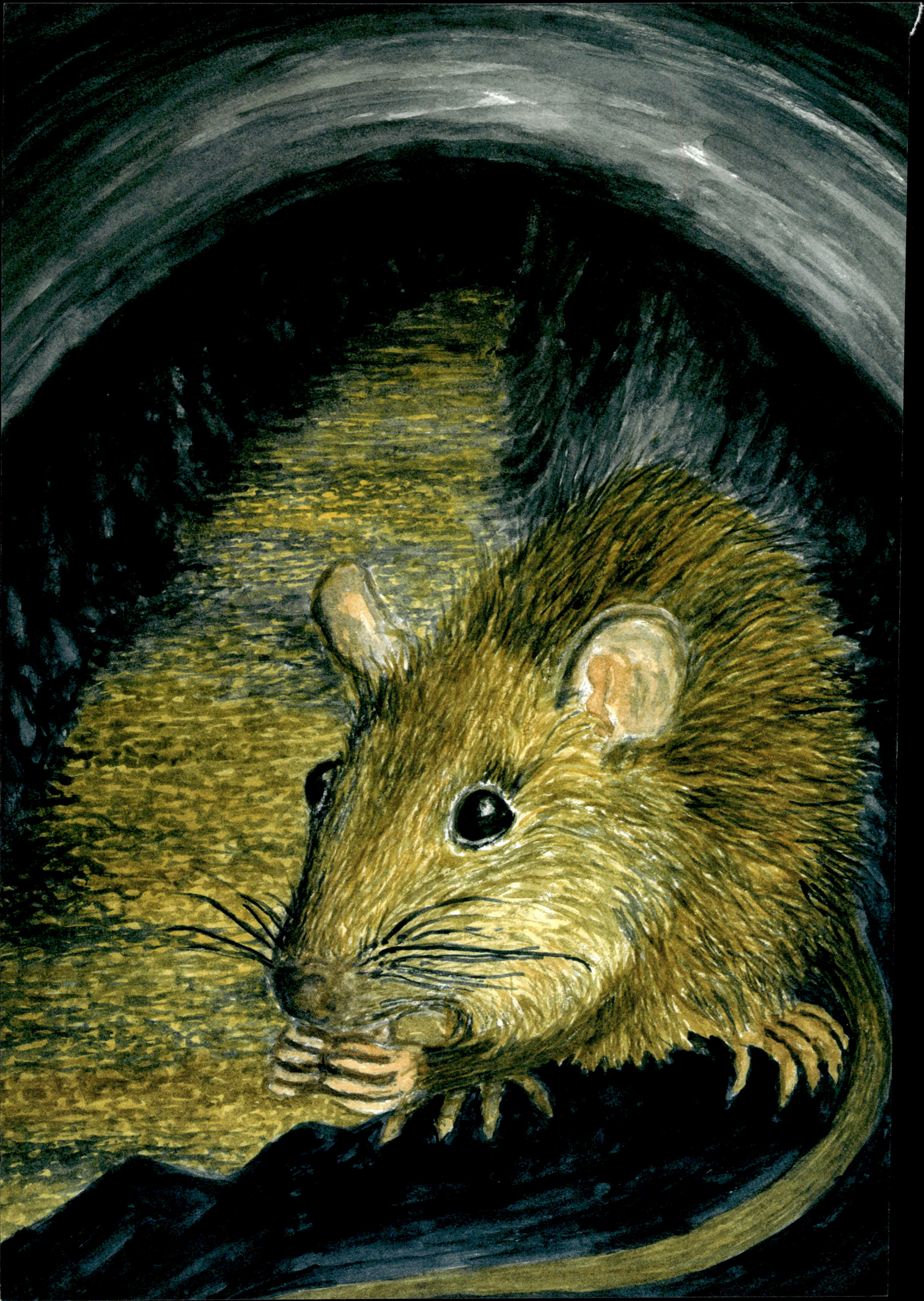

A Rat's Life

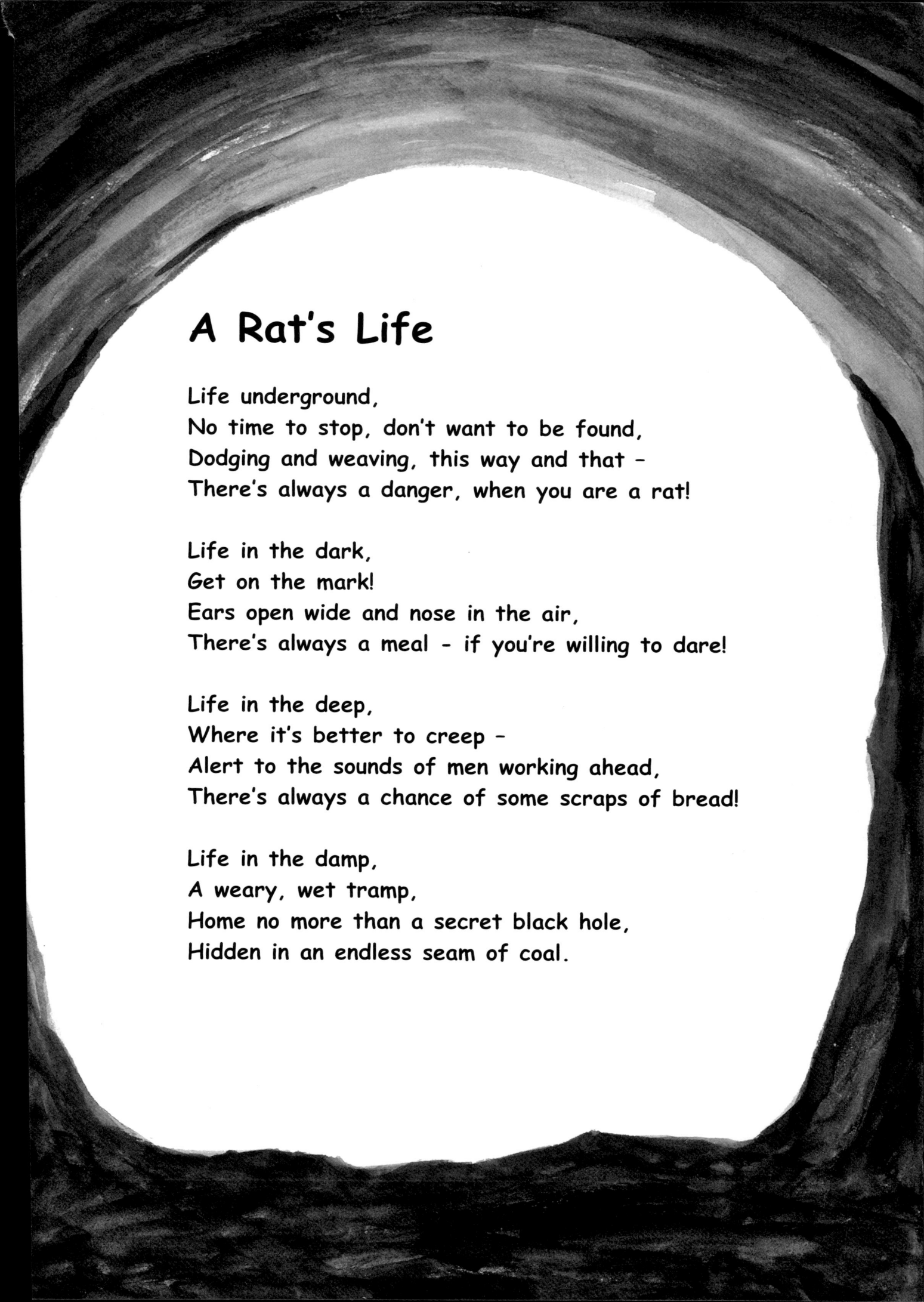

Life underground,
No time to stop, don't want to be found,
Dodging and weaving, this way and that –
There's always a danger, when you are a rat!

Life in the dark,
Get on the mark!
Ears open wide and nose in the air,
There's always a meal - if you're willing to dare!

Life in the deep,
Where it's better to creep –
Alert to the sounds of men working ahead,
There's always a chance of some scraps of bread!

Life in the damp,
A weary, wet tramp,
Home no more than a secret black hole,
Hidden in an endless seam of coal.

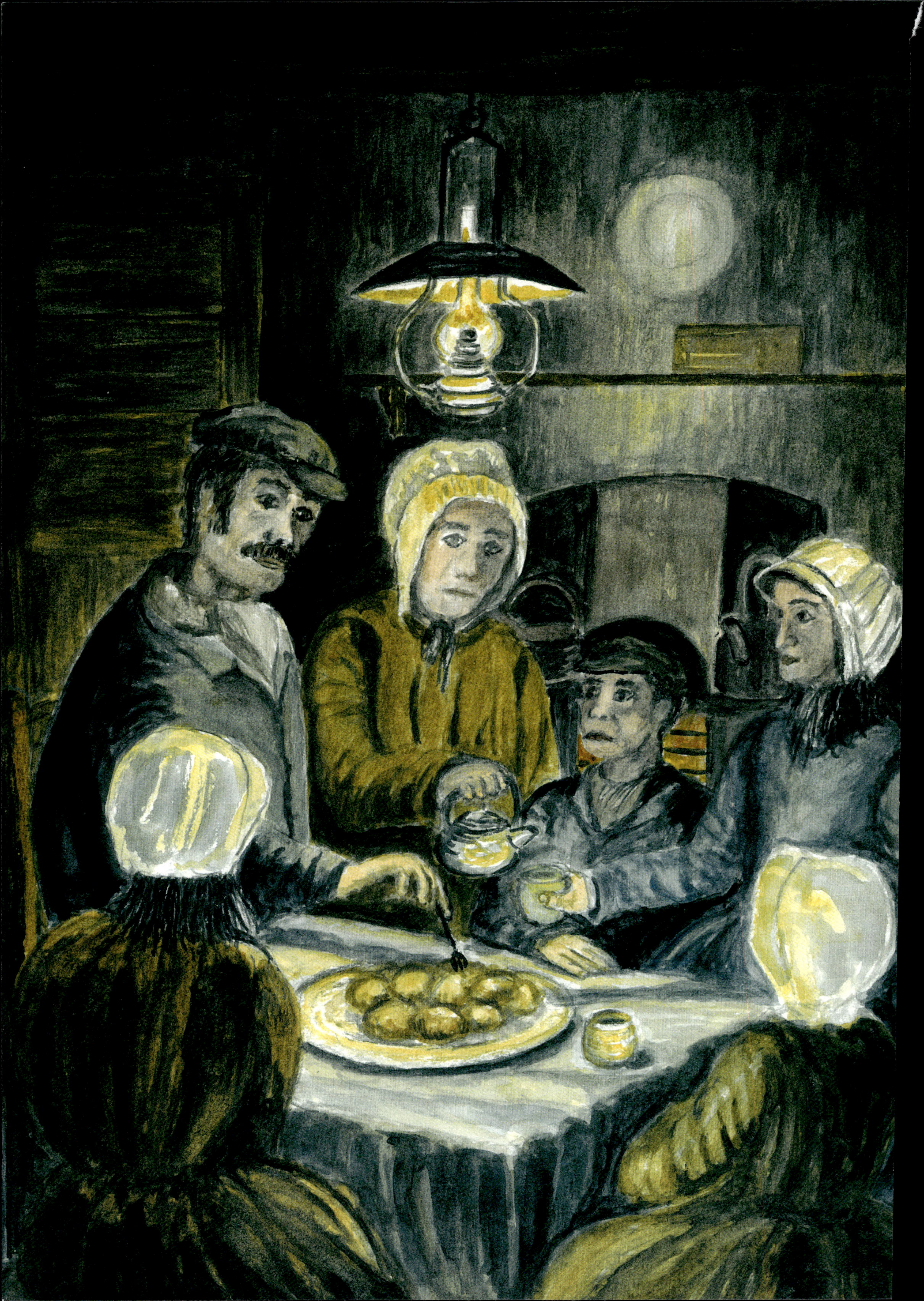

If There's No Work Tomorrow!

Gloom hangs over the evening meal,
Bleak news throughout the village,
Men to be laid off at the pit -
Will there be work tomorrow?

Boiled potatoes and not much more,
The pantry and cupboards are bare,
How much longer can we last?
If there's no work tomorrow!

Money for rent, is all but spent,
Just pennies left in the jar,
It may be that we have to beg,
If there's no work tomorrow!

Coal on the fire, is all but burnt,
Coalhouse and scuttle are empty,
How will we keep out the freezing cold?
If there's no work tomorrow!

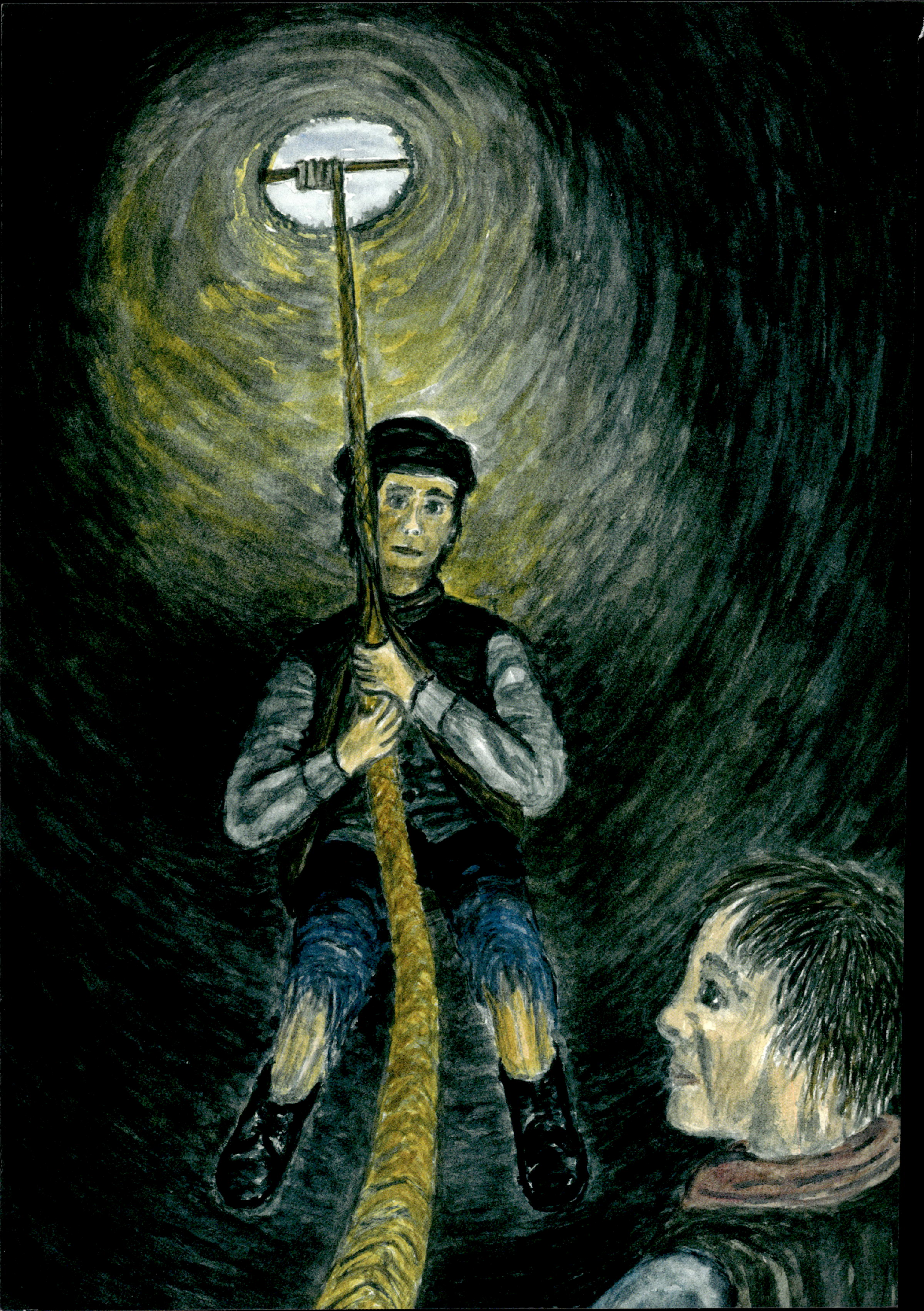

The Ascent

Above
A glimpse of light,
Sometimes blinking,
As if the pit is but an eye,
Within the Earth.

I catch the rope,
It tightens,
Creaking and groaning ...
As the weight bites.

I grip tensely,
Holding its rough, yellow fibres to my chest,
Feeling its strength
Praying that it wont break today.

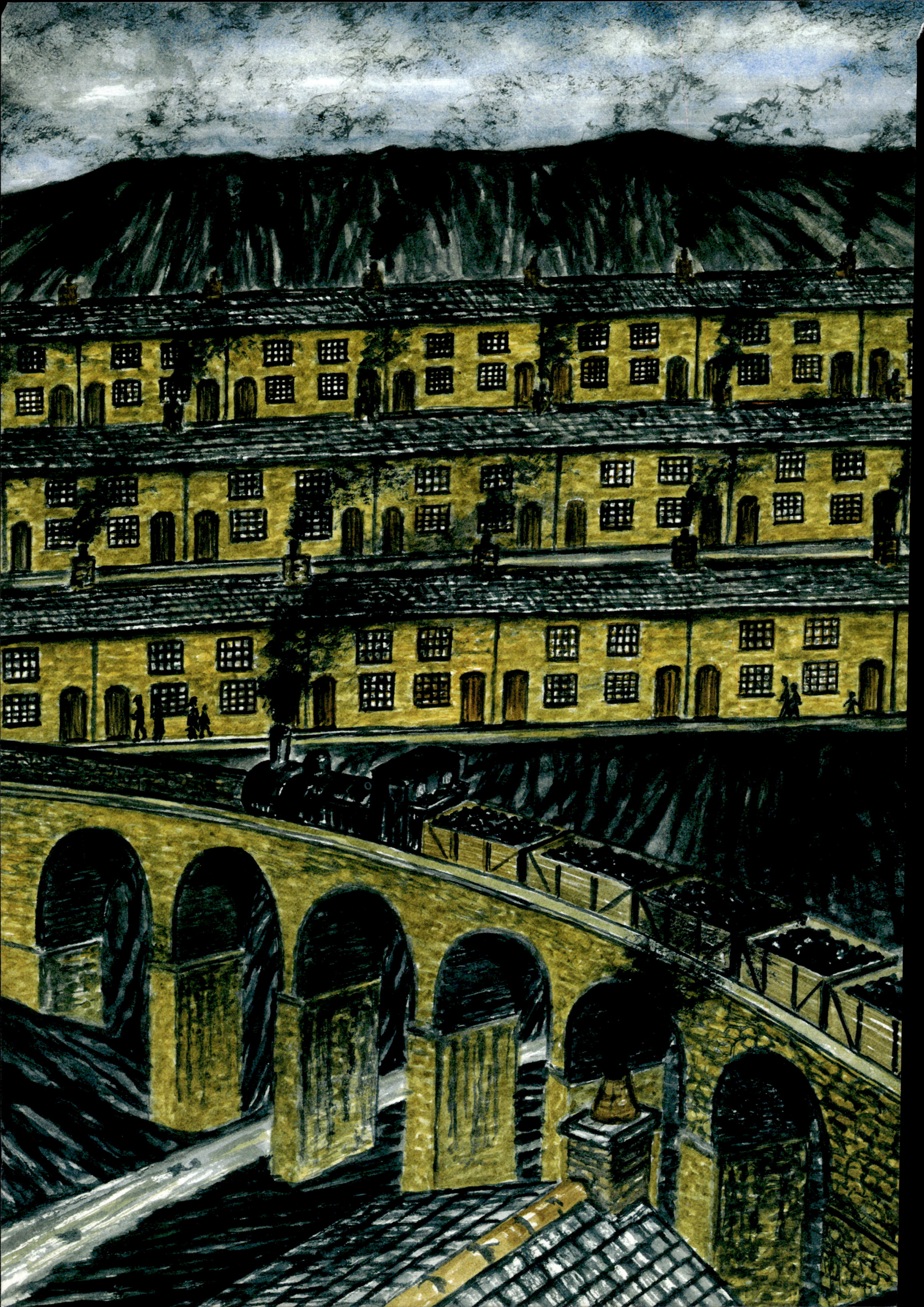

In The Shadow Of The Coal Tip

In the shadow of the coal tip, houses set along a row,
Terrace upon terrace, they grow and grow,
Built to last from old Welsh slate and random stone,
Each one a miner's castle, where no one stands alone.

Fire in the front room, kettle on the boil,
Tin bath on the rag mat after a day of toil,
Queen Victoria's portrait looks out at one and all,
Beside 'God Bless Our House' on a plate hung on the wall.

Hissing steam and whistling, coal trains thunder down the track,
Every window rattles, even windows on the back,
A hundred chimneys smoking make a dull and dirty sky,
Except for Monday morning when the washing's out to dry.

In the shadow of the coal tip, children play along their street,
Their tiny footsteps echo from the clogs upon their feet,
Busy mothers struggle to provide, make do and mend,
All of life a challenge from the chores that never end.

The Coal Master

The wealth of the land is in my hand,
An army of miners at my command,
Ready and able to do my willing,
Freeing the coal and earning a shilling!

Journey after journey, with never a stop,
Dram after dram, hauled to the top,
Hacked out, cut out, in pillar and stall,
But I'll give no pay if the coal's too small.

Coal for the furnace, that's never kept waiting,
Coal for the steam, for an engine that's racing,
Coal for a Nation and Empire in making,
Coal for a fortune, that's mine for the taking!

I make the future
And the future is coal!

Glossary

Coal Face – The part of the mine where miners cut and remove the coal.

Coal Dram – A wagon used for carrying coal.

Davy Lamp – A special safety lamp for use in mines. A Davy Lamp could also be used to show the presence of dangerous gasses.

Door Boy, Door Girl or Trapper – A child worker employed underground to open and close air doors to allow the movement of coal drams.

Haulier – A haulier was in charge of a pit pony.

Old Monmouthshire – Nickname given by the miners of Gwent for the roof a mine.

Roadway – Underground passage way. Roadways could stretch for miles underground.

The Author

Tomos is the pen name of Tom Maloney. The author is a native of Pontypool, South Wales and has been interested in the history of mining since an early age.

After studying Fine Art at Reading University he became a primary school teacher and continues to work as an Education Consultant.

The poetry and illustrations of the Pit Pony's Tale reflect his twin passions for heritage and education.

Primary School Resources

'The Victorians Underground'

'The Victorians Underground' is a fully planned and resourced Key Stage 2 education pack that has been produced by the author to support 'The Pit Pony's Tale'.

It is freely available to download from the National Grid for Learning (NGFL Wales) using the following link -

http://www.ngfl-cymru.org.uk/eng/ks2-victorians-underground